DUMP & BAKE

Desserts

Mix & Bake in the Same Pan!

Whether you're layering the ingredients or stirring them together, all the action takes place in your baking pan. No dirty bowls to wash and no electric mixer needed. Clean-up will be finished before your dessert is even out of the oven. It's a sweet way to bake!

Printed in China

Distributed By:

 Products

507 Industrial Street
Waverly, IA 50677

ISBN-13: 978-1-56383-494-3

Helpful Hints

✧ Glass or nonstick metal baking pans work well for these recipes.

✧ Use a fork to break up any lumps in dry ingredients (like cake mixes) before mixing.

✧ Pour liquid ingredients into the pan slowly and stir gently to avoid messes.

✧ When a recipe calls for melted butter, simply microwave it in a glass measuring cup.

✧ Use a rubber scraper to get dry ingredients out of pan corners and mix thoroughly.

✧ Before baking, scrape batter off the sides of pan and wipe off edges.

✧ Spread layers or batters evenly in the pan for uniform baking.

✧ To remove desserts easily from the pan, run a sharp knife around the edges to loosen while still warm, and then finish cooling as directed.

One pan is all it takes! What could be easier than that?

Wacky Chocolate Cake

1½ C. flour

1 C. sugar

¼ C. unsweetened cocoa powder

½ tsp. salt

1 tsp. baking soda

1 T. white vinegar

⅓ C. vegetable or light olive oil

1 tsp. vanilla

1 C. cold water*

Preheat oven to 350°.
  Grease an 8 x 8˝ baking pan.

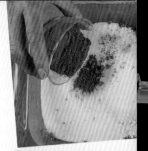

Mix it

Dump flour, sugar, cocoa powder, salt, and baking soda into prepared pan. Whisk together until evenly blended.

Make three wells in *flour* mixture. Pour vinegar into the first well.

Pour oil into the second well and vanilla into the last one.

Pour water over everything and whisk together well, scraping down sides and corners.

Bake it

35 to 40 minutes or until cake springs back when lightly touched in the center. Cool at least 5 minutes before cutting.

Serve it

warm with ice cream and fresh fruit, whipped topping, or a sprinkling of powdered sugar.

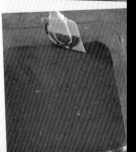

For mocha flavor, mix ½ C. cold brewed coffee and ½ C. cold water for the liquid.

Apricot Crumbles

1 C. butter, sliced

⅓ C. sugar

¼ C. brown sugar

1 egg yolk

1 tsp. vanilla

2 C. flour

1 tsp. baking powder

⅛ tsp. salt

¾ C. apricot jam or preserves

Fresh gingerroot

Preheat oven to 375°.
Use an ungreased 8 x 8˝ baking pan.

Mix it

Slice butter into baking pan and let soften. Add sugar and brown sugar; mash with a fork until well blended. Stir in egg yolk and vanilla.

Dump flour, baking powder, and salt into pan; stir until crumbly, working with hands as needed.

Remove and set aside ½ cup dough mixture. Press remaining dough into bottom of pan and up sides to form a shallow rim.

Spread jam over crust. Grate about 1 teaspoon gingerroot evenly over jam layer.

Crumble set-aside dough over the top.

Bake it

30 to 35 minutes or until golden brown. Cool at least 20 minutes before cutting.

Serve it

warm or at room temperature.

Banana Chocolate Nut Cake

½ C. butter

1 C. brown sugar

1 tsp. vanilla

1 egg

1 ripe banana

½ tsp. ground cinnamon

1½ C. flour

¾ tsp. baking soda

½ tsp. salt

1 C. dark chocolate chips

½ C. chopped walnuts

Preheat oven to 350°.
  Use an ungreased 9˝ round cake pan.

Mix it

Place butter in baking pan and set in
  oven to melt, 3 to 5 minutes.

Stir in brown sugar and vanilla.
  Let cool for 5 minutes. Add egg
  and whisk together until smooth
  and glossy.

Slice banana into baking pan and add
  cinnamon. Mash up banana with a
  fork and stir well.

Stir in half the flour with all the baking
  soda and salt. Stir in remaining flour
  until well blended.

Stir in chocolate chips and walnuts.
  Scrape down sides and spread batter
  evenly in pan.

Bake it

25 to 30 minutes or until golden
  brown and cake tests almost done
  with a toothpick. Let cool at least
  15 minutes before slicing.

Serve it

warm or at room temperature,
  topped with whipped cream and
  banana slices.

5-Layer Chocolate Chip Cookie Bars

1 (16.5 oz.) tube refrigerated chocolate chip cookie dough, softened

1 (14 oz.) can sweetened condensed milk

1 (11 to 12 oz.) bag white or butterscotch baking chips

1 C. sweetened flaked coconut

1 C. chopped pecans or walnuts

Preheat oven to 350°.
  Lightly grease a 9 x 13˝ baking pan.

Mix it

Press dough evenly into bottom of prepared pan and slightly up sides to form a shallow rim.

Bake for 15 minutes.

Drizzle sweetened condensed milk evenly over partially baked crust.

Sprinkle with baking chips, coconut, and nuts.

Bake it

about 25 minutes more or until golden brown. Let cool for 20 minutes before loosening bars from sides of pan. Cool completely before cutting.

Serve it

with a cup of coffee or glass of milk.

Easy Apple Toffee Tart

1 refrigerated pie crust (from a 14.1 oz. pkg.), softened

⅔ C. toffee bits, divided

2 to 3 large tart apples (such as Granny Smith)

2 T. sugar

1 T. cornstarch

¼ tsp. ground cinnamon

⅛ tsp. ground nutmeg

Water

1 tsp. coarse sugar

Preheat oven to 400°.
  Use an ungreased cookie sheet.

Mix it

Unroll pie crust on the cookie sheet. Sprinkle ⅓ cup toffee bits over center of crust and press lightly.

Peel and thinly slice the apples over the toffee bits, leaving outer 2″ of crust uncovered. Sprinkle 2 tablespoons sugar, cornstarch, cinnamon, and nutmeg evenly over apples; toss lightly with a fork.

Sprinkle remaining ⅓ cup toffee bits over apples.

Fold and pleat edge of crust around apples to form a rim that holds fruit. Brush crust with water and sprinkle with coarse sugar.

Bake it

25 to 30 minutes or until crust is golden brown. Cool slightly.

Serve it

warm or at room temperature with vanilla or cinnamon ice cream and a sprinkling of powdered sugar.

Cherry Cheesecake Cookie Pizza

1 (16.5 oz.) tube sugar cookie dough, softened

1 C. marshmallow creme

2 C. ready-to-eat cheesecake filling
(from a 24.3 oz. tub)

1 (21 oz.) can cherry pie filling

¾ C. ready-to-use vanilla frosting

½ C. sliced almonds, optional

Preheat oven to 350°.
  Lightly grease a 12˝ pizza pan.

Mix it

Press cookie dough into prepared pizza pan, forming a rim around edge.

Bake it

18 to 23 minutes or until lightly browned around edge. Let crust cool completely.

Spread marshmallow creme over crust. Spread cheesecake filling over marshmallow creme layer.

Spread pie filling on top, stopping ½˝ from edge of crust.

Spoon frosting into a pastry bag fitted with a large star tip and pipe frosting around edge of cookie crust. Sprinkle almonds on top, if desired. Refrigerate before cutting into wedges.

Serve it

cold. It's cherry good!

Just Peachy Cobbler

6 T. butter

½ C. brown sugar

1 C. flour

1½ tsp. baking powder

½ tsp. salt

½ tsp. ground cinnamon

½ C. buttermilk

¼ C. half & half

3 C. sliced fresh or frozen (thawed) peaches

Coarse sugar, optional

Preheat oven to 325°.
Use an ungreased 9 x 9˝ baking pan.

Mix it

Place butter in baking pan and set in
oven to melt, 3 to 5 minutes. Brush
butter over bottom and sides of pan.

Dump brown sugar, flour, baking
powder, salt, and cinnamon into pan
and stir together until combined.
Make a well in the center.

Add buttermilk and half & half. Whisk
until smooth and well blended,
scraping down sides. Spread batter
evenly in pan.

Arrange peaches over batter. Sprinkle
with coarse sugar, if desired.

Bake it

55 to 60 minutes or until lightly
browned. Let cool at least 10 minutes
before cutting.

Serve it

warm or cold with whipped topping or
scoops of cinnamon ice cream.

Fudgy Skillet Brownies

¼ C. butter

¼ C. heavy cream

8 oz. bittersweet chocolate, chopped

1¼ C. sugar

3 eggs

1 C. flour

¼ C. unsweetened cocoa powder

½ tsp. salt

Preheat oven to 350°.
  Use an ungreased 9˝ to 10˝
  ovenproof nonstick skillet.

Mix it

Place butter and cream in skillet
  over medium heat; stir and bring
  to a simmer.

Reduce heat to medium-low and add
  chocolate. Cook until chocolate is
  melted, stirring constantly. Remove
  from heat and let cool to room
  temperature.

Stir sugar and eggs into chocolate
  mixture; mix well.

Fold in flour, cocoa powder, and
  salt until well combined. Scrape
  down sides and spread batter
  evenly in skillet.

Bake it

about 40 minutes or until brownies
  test done with a toothpick. Let cool.

Serve it

warm or at room temperature. Drizzle
  with thinned chocolate icing or top
  with ice cream before serving.

Very Berry Cheesecake Squares

½ C. butter

1 C. flour

½ C. powdered sugar

⅛ tsp. salt

2 (8 oz.) tubs mixed berry whipped cream cheese

¼ C. strawberry preserves

1 C. fresh blueberries

1 C. fresh red raspberries

1 (8 oz.) tub frozen whipped topping, thawed

Preheat oven to 350°.
Grease an 8 x 8˝ baking pan.

Mix it

Slice butter into prepared pan and let soften.

Dump flour, powdered sugar, and salt into pan. Mash with a fork until well mixed and crumbly. Press mixture into bottom of pan.

Bake it

about 18 minutes or until edges begin to brown. Let cool for 5 minutes.

Spread cream cheese over warm crust. Bake 15 to 20 minutes more, until filling is set. Cool completely, about 2 hours.

Spread preserves over filling. Sprinkle blueberries and raspberries on top.

Spread whipped topping over everything and chill at least 2 hours before serving.

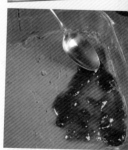

Serve it

with additional fresh berries sprinkled on top, if desired.

Caramel Coconut Squares

½ C. butter

1 C. sugar

1½ C. flour

½ tsp. baking powder

½ tsp. baking soda

¼ tsp. salt

1 egg

1 T. vanilla

12 caramels, unwrapped

¼ C. mini chocolate chips

1 C. sweetened flaked coconut

Preheat oven to 350°.
Use an ungreased 9 x 9˝ baking pan.

Mix it

Slice butter into baking pan and set in oven to melt, about 3 minutes.

Stir sugar into butter. Let cool for 5 minutes.

Dump flour, baking powder, baking soda, and salt into pan. Stir to combine.

Make a well in the center. Add egg and vanilla; stir everything together, scraping down sides. Press mixture into pan.

Cut caramels into small pieces and scatter over dough. Sprinkle chocolate chips and coconut on top.

Bake it

12 to 16 minutes or until crust and coconut are golden brown. Cool slightly before cutting into squares.

Serve it

warm and drizzle pieces with caramel topping, if desired.

Strawberry Cake

1 (18.25 oz.) pkg. white or yellow cake mix

1 (3.4 oz.) pkg. French vanilla instant
pudding mix, divided

3 eggs

¼ C. vegetable oil

¾ C. water

1 (21 oz.) can strawberry pie filling

1 (8 oz.) tub frozen whipped topping, thawed

3 T. milk

Preheat oven to 325°.
  Lightly grease a 9 x 13˝ baking pan.

Mix it

Dump cake mix and 2 tablespoons
pudding mix into prepared pan.
Stir together and make a well in
the center.

Add eggs, oil, and water; whisk until
well blended, scraping down sides.

Spoon pie filling over batter and
fold together gently. Spread batter
evenly in pan, swirling lightly.

Bake it

about 40 minutes or until cake
tests done with a toothpick.
Cool completely. Stir remaining
pudding mix into whipped topping
until combined; stir in milk until
well blended and let stand
5 to 10 minutes. Stir again
and spread mixture over cake.
Refrigerate until serving.

Serve it

with fresh strawberries on top.

Skillet Sugar Cookie

1 (17.5 oz.) pouch sugar cookie mix
1 egg
½ C. cold butter
1 C. mini M&Ms

Preheat oven to 350°.
  Oil a 10˝ cast iron skillet.

Mix it

Dump cookie mix into prepared skillet and make a well in the center.

Add egg and grate butter over everything.

Mash together with a fork and stir until dough forms and mixture is well blended. Work with hands as needed.

Stir in M&Ms.

Press dough into skillet, scraping down sides.

Bake it

25 to 30 minutes or until set and lightly browned. Let cool before slicing.

Serve it

warm or at room temperature. If desired, drizzle pieces with thinned vanilla frosting.

Sopapilla Cheesecake Dessert

2 (8 oz.) tubes refrigerated crescent rolls or seamless
dough sheets, divided

3 (8 oz.) tubs cream cheese spread, softened

1¾ C. sugar, divided

2 tsp. vanilla

½ C. butter, melted

1 tsp. ground cinnamon, or to taste

¼ C. sliced almonds

Preheat oven to 350°.
  Use an ungreased 9 x 13˝ baking pan.

Mix it

Unroll one tube of dough and press into bottom of baking pan and slightly up sides for bottom crust.

Spread cream cheese over crust and sprinkle evenly with 1¼ cups sugar. Drizzle with vanilla.

Unroll remaining tube of dough; flatten to 9 x 13˝ and place over filling to cover completely.

Drizzle butter over top crust; spread evenly. Sprinkle with remaining ½ cup sugar and cinnamon.

Scatter almonds over the top.

Bake it

40 to 45 minutes or until puffy and golden brown. Cool completely in the pan before cutting.

Serve it

at room temperature. Drizzle pieces with honey, if desired.

Impossible
Buttermilk Pie

3 eggs
1 C. buttermilk
⅓ C. butter, melted
1 tsp. vanilla
1⅓ C. sugar
¾ C. biscuit baking mix
Pinch of ground nutmeg

Preheat oven to 350°.
Grease a 9˝ deep dish pie plate.

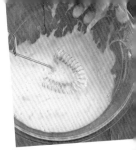

Mix it

Break eggs into prepared pie plate and whisk thoroughly.

Add buttermilk, butter, and vanilla; whisk together well.

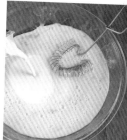

Dump sugar, baking mix, and nutmeg into pie plate and whisk everything together for 3 to 5 minutes, until smooth and well blended. Scrape down sides.

Bake it

35 to 40 minutes or until lightly browned and still a little jiggly in the center. Let cool before slicing into wedges. Chill before serving, if desired.

Serve it

at room temperature or chilled. Sprinkle with powdered sugar and nutmeg or top with fresh fruit.

Hot Fudge Sundae Cake

1 C. flour

¾ C. sugar

2 T. plus ¼ C. unsweetened cocoa powder, divided

2 tsp. baking powder

¼ tsp. salt

½ C. milk

2 T. vegetable oil

1 tsp. vanilla

¾ to 1 C. chopped walnuts

1 C. brown sugar

1¾ C. hot water

Preheat oven to 350°.
Use an ungreased 9 x 9″ baking pan.

Mix it

Dump flour, sugar, 2 tablespoons cocoa powder, baking powder, and salt into baking pan and whisk together.

Make a well in the center and stir in milk, oil, and vanilla with a fork until smooth.

Stir in walnuts, scraping down sides. Spread batter evenly in pan.

Sprinkle with brown sugar and remaining ¼ cup cocoa powder.

Pour hot water over everything (do not stir).

Bake it

about 40 minutes. Let stand a few minutes and then loosen cake from sides of pan. Let cool for 15 minutes before cutting.

Serve it

promptly by inverting each piece onto a dessert plate. Top with remaining sauce from pan, whipped topping, and a maraschino cherry.

Rhubarb Betty

5 to 6 C. chopped fresh or frozen (thawed) rhubarb

¾ C. sugar

2 tsp. ground cinnamon

6 slices Texas toast (crusts removed), cubed

¼ C. butter, melted

Cinnamon sugar

Preheat oven to 350°.
Use an ungreased 9 x 13˝ baking pan.

Mix it

Toss together rhubarb, sugar, and cinnamon in baking pan until evenly coated.

Add half the bread cubes and toss lightly.

Top with remaining bread cubes and drizzle with butter.

Sprinkle with cinnamon sugar to taste. Cover with foil.

Bake it

about 40 minutes or until rhubarb is tender and bubbly. Uncover and bake 5 to 10 minutes more to crisp up bread.

Serve it

warm with ice cream.

Make **Apple Betty** *by using chopped apples in place of rhubarb and 4 to 5 cups cubed cinnamon swirl bread in place of Texas toast. Reduce the amount of cinnamon in recipe to taste.*

Pumpkin Crisp

1 (15 oz.) can pumpkin puree

1 (12 oz.) can evaporated milk

3 eggs

1 C. sugar

2 tsp. ground cinnamon

1 (18.25 oz.) pkg. yellow cake mix

1 C. chopped pecans

½ C. toffee bits, optional

1 C. butter, melted

Preheat oven to 350°.
  Grease a 9 x 13˝ baking pan.

Mix it

Dump pumpkin puree into prepared pan. Add evaporated milk, eggs, sugar, and cinnamon. Whisk together until well blended, scraping down sides.

Sprinkle cake mix over pumpkin mixture.

Sprinkle pecans over cake mix and top with toffee bits, if desired.

Drizzle butter over everything.

Bake it

50 to 55 minutes or until set and golden brown. Let cool before cutting.

Serve it

at room temperature or chilled with a dollop of ready-to-use cream cheese frosting on each piece.

Peanut Butter Bars

½ C. butter

½ C. sugar

½ C. brown sugar

½ C. creamy peanut butter

1 egg

1 tsp. vanilla

1 C. flour

½ C. quick-cooking oats

1 tsp. baking soda

¼ tsp. salt

1 C. chocolate chips

Preheat oven to 350°.
  Grease a 9 x 13˝ baking pan.

Mix it

Slice butter into prepared pan and set in oven to melt, about 3 minutes.

Remove pan from oven and add sugar, brown sugar, and peanut butter. Stir together until creamy, scraping down sides. Add egg and vanilla; whisk well.

Dump flour, oats, baking soda, and salt into baking pan. Stir everything together until well mixed. Press mixture into pan.

Sprinkle chocolate chips over the top.

Bake it

17 to 22 minutes or until lightly browned. Let cool before cutting.

Serve it

with a glass of milk.

Pineapple Cream Cake

1 (16.5 oz.) pkg. pineapple cake mix

1 (3.4 oz.) pkg. vanilla instant pudding mix

1 (20 oz.) can crushed pineapple, juice reserved

Water

3 eggs

Butter cookies

½ C. cold butter

Preheat oven to 325°.
  Grease a 9 x 13˝ baking pan.

Mix it

Dump cake mix and pudding mix
  into prepared pan. Make a well in
  the center.

Combine reserved juice from pineapple
  with enough water to measure
  1½ cups liquid. Add eggs and juice
  mixture to pan and whisk thoroughly.

Stir in pineapple. Scrape down sides
  and spread batter evenly in pan.

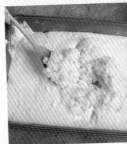

Crush cookies in a zippered plastic
  bag to measure ½ cup crumbs.

Slice butter and distribute evenly
  over cake batter. Sprinkle with
  cookie crumbs.

Bake it

40 to 45 minutes or until cake
  tests done with a toothpick. Cool
  completely and chill before slicing.

Serve it

with whipped cream and maraschino
  cherries on top.

Deep Dish Pumpkin Snack Cake

¾ C. butter

½ C. sugar

¾ C. brown sugar

1 egg

2 tsp. vanilla

½ C. pumpkin puree

1½ C. flour

1 tsp. baking soda

½ tsp. salt

2 tsp. pumpkin pie spice

1 C. semi-sweet chocolate chunks or chips

Preheat oven to 350°.
  Use an ungreased 10˝ ovenproof
  nonstick skillet.

Mix it

Slice butter into skillet and set over
  medium heat until melted.

Remove from heat and whisk in sugar
  and brown sugar; let cool slightly.

Whisk in egg and vanilla until light and
  well blended.

Stir in pumpkin puree and mix well.

Dump flour, baking soda, salt, and
  pie spice into skillet and whisk well,
  scraping down sides.

Stir in chocolate chunks. Spread batter
  evenly in skillet.

Bake it

25 to 30 minutes or until set and
  lightly browned around edges (do
  not overbake). Let cool in skillet.

Serve it

directly from skillet.

Peppermint Patty Brownies

1 (18.25 oz.) pkg. chocolate cake mix

1 egg

1 tsp. vanilla

½ C. butter, softened

25 small peppermint patties

½ C. sweetened condensed milk

½ C. dark or semi-sweet chocolate chips

Preheat oven to 350°.
  Lightly grease an 8 x 8˝ baking pan.

Mix it

Dump cake mix into prepared pan. Add egg, vanilla, and butter.

Mix well with a fork until crumbly. Remove and set aside 2 cups of dough mixture for topping. Press remaining dough into bottom of pan.

Unwrap peppermint patties and arrange them on top of dough in pan.

Flatten pieces of set-aside dough and place over peppermints to make a top crust.

Drizzle sweetened condensed milk evenly over the top. Sprinkle with chocolate chips.

Bake it

35 to 40 minutes, until puffy. Let cool for 20 minutes and then loosen bars from sides of pan. Cool completely before cutting (brownies flatten as they cool).

Serve it

with mint chip ice cream.

Reese's Brown Butter Skillet Cookie

1 C. butter

½ C. sugar

1 C. brown sugar

2 eggs

1 tsp. vanilla

½ tsp. salt

2½ C. flour

1 tsp. baking soda

1 C. mini semi-sweet chocolate chips

1¼ C. Reese's Pieces, divided

Preheat oven to 375°.
  Use an ungreased 10˝ cast iron skillet.

Mix it

Slice butter into skillet and place over medium heat; stir until melted and beginning to brown. Remove from heat and let cool to lukewarm.

Add sugar and brown sugar; whisk together well. Beat in eggs, vanilla, and salt until smooth.

Dump flour and baking soda into skillet and beat well, scraping down sides.

Stir in chocolate chips and ¾ cup Reese's Pieces.

Press dough into skillet. Sprinkle remaining ½ cup Reese's Pieces over the top and pat gently in place.

Bake it

25 to 35 minutes or until set and golden brown around edges. Cool before cutting.

Serve it

from the pan.

Snickers Pie

1½ C. flour

½ tsp. salt

1½ tsp. sugar

½ C. vegetable oil

2 T. milk or half & half

2 to 2½ C. ready-to-eat cheesecake filling (from a 24.3 oz. tub)

1 C. milk chocolate chips

¼ C. caramel topping

1 C. chopped peanuts, divided

1 (8 oz.) tub frozen whipped topping, thawed

1 (1.86 oz.) Snickers candy bar, chopped

Preheat oven to 425°.
Use an ungreased 9″ pie plate.

Mix it

To make no-roll crust,* dump flour, salt, and sugar into pie plate and stir. Make a well in the center; add oil and milk. Mix with a fork until dough forms. Press into pie plate and flute the edge. Poke holes in dough all over with a fork.

Bake it

10 to 13 minutes or until lightly browned. Let cool completely.

Spread cheesecake filling in cooled crust. Sprinkle with chocolate chips. Drizzle with caramel topping. Scatter ¾ cup peanuts on top and press lightly.

Spread whipped topping over pie. Sprinkle with remaining ¼ cup peanuts and Snickers pieces. Chill.

Serve it

cold. Yum!

Instead of making the no-roll crust, you may purchase and bake a ready-to-bake 9″ pie shell.

Mellow Yellow Poke Cake

1 (16.5 oz.) pkg. lemon cake mix

3 eggs

⅓ C. vegetable oil

12 oz. Mello Yello soda

1 (8 oz.) can crushed pineapple, drained

1 (14 oz.) can sweetened condensed milk

1 (8 oz.) tub frozen whipped topping, thawed

½ C. toasted or plain sweetened flaked coconut

Preheat oven to 350°.
  Grease a 9 x 13˝ baking pan.

Mix it

Dump cake mix into prepared pan and make a well in the center.

Add eggs, oil, and soda. Whisk until well blended, scraping down sides and corners.

Fold in pineapple and spread batter evenly in pan.

Bake it

as directed on package, 22 to 26 minutes, or until cake tests done with a toothpick. Remove from oven and let cool for 10 minutes.

With the handle of a wooden spoon, poke holes in warm cake. Drizzle sweetened condensed milk over cake, filling holes. Cool completely.

Spread whipped topping over cake and sprinkle with coconut. Refrigerate at least 2 hours before cutting.

Serve it

with picks of fresh pineapple chunks or maraschino cherries on top.

Apple Pie Snickerdoodle Bars

¼ C. sugar

2½ tsp. ground cinnamon, or to taste

1 (16.5 oz.) tube refrigerated sugar cookie dough, softened

1 (20 oz.) can apple pie filling

Preheat oven to 350°.
  Lightly grease a 9 x 9˝ baking pan.

Mix it

Combine sugar and cinnamon in a zippered plastic bag; seal bag and shake well. Set aside.

Press ⅔ of cookie dough into bottom of prepared pan.

Sprinkle evenly with 3 tablespoons sugar-cinnamon mixture.

Spread apple filling over cookie crust.

Flatten pieces of remaining cookie dough and arrange over apple layer like a top crust (some filling will peek through).

Sprinkle remaining sugar-cinnamon mixture over the top.

Bake it

35 to 40 minutes or until lightly browned. Let cool for 20 to 30 minutes before loosening bars from sides of pan. Cool completely before cutting.

Serve it

with a glass of cold milk.

Almond Snack Cake

1 C. sugar, plus extra for sprinkling

Zest of 1 lemon

2 eggs

¼ tsp. salt

½ tsp. vanilla

1 tsp. almond extract

1 C. flour

½ C. butter, melted and cooled

Sliced almonds

½ C. ready-to-use white frosting

Preheat oven to 350°.
  Butter a 9˝ round cake pan.

Mix it

Combine sugar and zest in prepared
  pan and toss together.

Add eggs, salt, vanilla, and almond
  extract; whisk together until
  well blended.

Stir in flour.

Add butter and stir until well mixed.
  Scrape down sides and spread
  batter evenly in pan.

Scatter almonds over the top and
  sprinkle lightly with sugar.

Bake it

22 to 27 minutes or until lightly
  browned. Let cool for 5 minutes
  before loosening cake from sides
  of pan. If desired, remove cake to a
  serving plate. Briefly warm frosting
  in the microwave and drizzle over
  cake before cutting.

Serve it

warm or at room temperature.

Carrot Cake

2 C. flour
2 tsp. baking powder
1½ tsp. baking soda
1 tsp. salt
1 T. ground cinnamon
1½ C. sugar
4 eggs

1¼ C. light olive oil
2 C. grated raw carrots
1 (8 oz.) can crushed
  pineapple, drained
½ C. raisins
½ C. chopped walnuts
Ready-to-use cream
  cheese frosting

Preheat oven to 350°.
  Grease a 9 x 13˝ nonstick baking pan.

Mix it

Dump flour, baking powder, baking
  soda, salt, and cinnamon into
  prepared pan and stir together.
  Make a well in the center.

Add sugar, eggs, and oil; whisk
  together well.

Fold in carrots, pineapple, raisins,
  and walnuts. Scrape down sides and
  corners; spread batter evenly in pan.

Bake it

40 to 45 minutes or until a toothpick
  inserted near center comes out
  almost clean. Let cool completely.
  Spread frosting over cake.

Serve it

at room temperature or chilled.

Nut Roll Bars

1 (18.25 oz.) pkg. yellow cake mix
1 egg
¼ C. butter, melted
1 (10 oz.) pkg. peanut butter chips
1 C. crisp rice cereal
½ C. light corn syrup
3 C. mini marshmallows
1½ C. salted peanuts, chopped

Preheat oven to 350°.
  Use an ungreased 9 x 13˝ baking pan.

Mix it

Dump cake mix into baking pan and
make a well in the center. Add egg
and butter; stir or work with hands
until well mixed. Press dough into pan.

Bake it

11 to 14 minutes. Remove from oven
and sprinkle peanut butter chips
and cereal over crust. Drizzle
evenly with corn syrup. Top with
marshmallows and peanuts, pressing
peanuts down lightly.

Return to oven and bake 5 to 7 minutes
more or until marshmallows are
puffy and just beginning to brown.
Remove from oven and gently press
down on peanuts to set. Let cool
before cutting.

Serve it

at room temperature.

French Pear Tart

Flour

1 sheet frozen puff pastry, thawed (from a 17.3 oz. pkg.)

½ C. sugar

1½ tsp. apple cider vinegar

2 T. water

2 T. butter

3 firm Bartlett or Anjou pears, peeled and cored

Lemon juice

Preheat oven to 375°.
Use an ugreased 10˝ cast iron skillet.

Mix it

On a floured surface, unfold pastry and roll out large enough to cut an 11˝ circle (cut around a dinner plate). Cover and refrigerate dough circle; discard scraps.

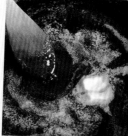

In the skillet over medium heat, mix sugar, vinegar, and water. Cook without stirring until golden, 10 to 12 minutes. Stir in butter.

Cut each pear into six wedges and dip in lemon juice; drain on paper towels. Fan out wedges in skillet as shown. Cover and cook until pears are crisp-tender, 10 to 15 minutes. Remove from heat.

Place pastry over pears, tucking edge under. Set a pot lid directly on pastry.

Bake it

15 minutes. Remove lid and bake 15 minutes more, until golden. Let cool in skillet for 15 minutes. Loosen pastry from skillet and carefully invert dessert onto a serving plate.

Serve it

promptly, topped with whipped cream.

serves 20

Raspberry Crumb Bars

2 C. flour

1½ C. old-fashioned oats

1 C. brown sugar

1 tsp. ground cinnamon

½ tsp. salt

1 C. cold butter

1 C. sliced almonds

1 (15.25 oz.) jar seedless raspberry
   fruit spread

62

Preheat oven to 325°.
Use an ungreased 9 x 13˝ baking pan.

Mix it

Dump flour, oats, brown sugar, cinnamon, and salt into baking pan and stir together.

Grate butter over oat mixture; stir until blended. Work with hands until mixture is crumbly and holds together. Stir in almonds. Remove 1½ cups crumb mixture and chill until later. Press remaining mixture into bottom of pan.

Bake it

about 25 minutes or until almonds begin to brown. Let cool for 20 minutes.

Spoon fruit spread evenly over crust, stopping ½˝ from edges. Sprinkle with chilled crumbs.

Return to oven and bake 32 to 37 minutes more, until lightly browned and bubbly. Cool slightly before loosening bars from sides of pan. Cool completely before cutting.

Serve it

like bars or with ice cream and fresh raspberries.

Index